100 QUESTIONS about SHARKS

and all the answers too!

Written and Illustrated by
Simon Abbott

PETER PAUPER PRESS, INC.
White Plains, New York

For Casey and Wesley
Happy surfing!

PETER PAUPER PRESS

In 1928, at the age of twenty-two, Peter Beilenson began printing books on a small press in the basement of his parents' home in Larchmont, New York. Peter—and later, his wife, Edna—sought to create fine books that sold at "prices even a pauper could afford."

Today, still family owned and operated, Peter Pauper Press continues to honor our founders' legacy of quality, value, and fun for big kids and small kids alike.

Designed by Heather Zschock

Text and illustrations copyright © 2019 by Simon Abbott

Published by Peter Pauper Press, Inc.
202 Mamaroneck Avenue
White Plains, New York 10601 USA

Published in the United Kingdom and Europe by Peter Pauper Press, Inc.
c/o White Pebble International
Unit 2, Plot 11 Terminus Rd.
Chichester, West Sussex PO19 8TX, UK

Library of Congress Cataloging-in-Publication Data Available

ISBN 978-1-4413-3107-6
Manufactured for Peter Pauper Press, Inc.
Printed in China

7 6 5 4 3

Visit us at www.peterpauper.com

WELCOME!

Are you ready to leap into the wonderful world of sharks?

Which shark swims the fastest?

What is a shark's skeleton made of?

How strong is a shark's jaw?

Let's speed along the seabed and discover the answers to these questions, as well as more fin-tastic facts!

THE SHARK'S FAMILY TREE

**If you thought dinosaurs were the planet's oldest creatures, think again!
Let's see where sharks sit on the ancient animal timeline.**

How old are sharks?
These creatures have been swimming in our oceans for over 420 million
years. That beats the dinosaurs by nearly 200 million years!

How do we know this?
Fossils: the remains of plants or animals that lived a long time ago,
preserved in rocks. Although the soft skeleton of a shark doesn't fossilize
easily, their scales, fin spines, and teeth do. These fossils give us lots of
information about prehistoric sharks, even their last meals!

What are the oldest shark fossils that have been discovered?

The 420 million-year-old scales found in Siberia and Mongolia are the oldest fossils that belonged to the ancestors of modern-day sharks.

How did sharks outlast animals like the T-rex or plesiosaurus?

Huge environmental changes, perhaps due to volcanic explosions or a comet impact, have at times wiped out 95 percent of Earth's species. Sharks survived by being adaptable. Their fins and torpedo-like bodies allowed them to speed through water and catch their prey. Some species developed tough armor-like scales for protection, and they evolved a flexible jaw to munch on creatures larger than themselves. As oxygen levels dropped, sharks retreated to the dark ocean depths, with some developing the ability to glow in the dark!

Which shark is the oldest?
At 380 million years old, the **Cladoselache** *(CLAD-oh-sell-ah-kee)*, or **scaleless shark** is seen as the first "true shark." It had a fish-shaped head, and a long, lean body.

Which prehistoric shark wins the First Prize Feeder award?
That title goes to the appropriately named **shell crusher shark**, or **Ptychodus** *(TIH-coh-dus)*. This creature crunched through huge amounts of shellfish with its mighty jaw and an incredible 550 giant, flat teeth.

Time to get out the tape measure!
Which ancient specimen grabs the Super-Sized Shark trophy?
The largest known shark ever to swim Earth's oceans is the awesome **megalodon** *(MEG-ah-low-don)*. This colossal creature had a jaw full of teeth as long as pencils, and measured up to 60 feet (18 m) from nose to tail. That's as long as a bowling alley!

Which strange-looking shark wins the Ancient Oddball honor?
That prize goes to the male **Stethacanthus** *(STETH-ah-CAN-thus)* shark. These bizarre-looking creatures had spikes on their snouts, whips on their fins, and an extraordinary anvil-shaped dorsal fin. We don't know what these features were for, but I'm not hanging around to ask them!

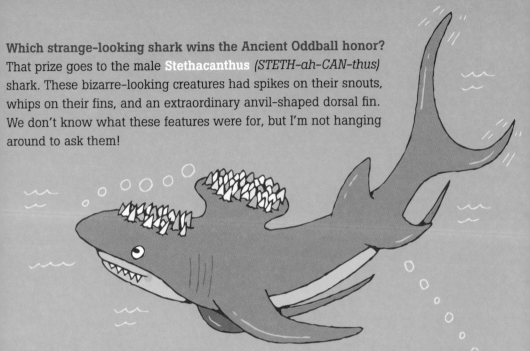

Which shark snags the Best Bite title?
The horrific-looking **Helicoprion** *(HEE-lih-coh-PRY-on)*. This marine monster had a buzz saw-shaped spiral of teeth fixed in its lower jaw. These teeth would be constantly replaced, with razor-sharp new additions pushing out the old ones.

FROM TIP TO TAIL!

Let's investigate a shark's fantastic features, and find out how this special sea creature operates.

What are the fins on top for?
Most sharks have 2 **dorsal fins** on their backs, which help them to balance as they swim.

What about the fins on the bottom?
These fins, the **pectoral** and **pelvic fins**, help the shark to steer, push itself up in the water, and keep itself from rolling over. Some species, such as the angelshark, live on the seabed and use their pectoral fins to move themselves across the ocean floor.

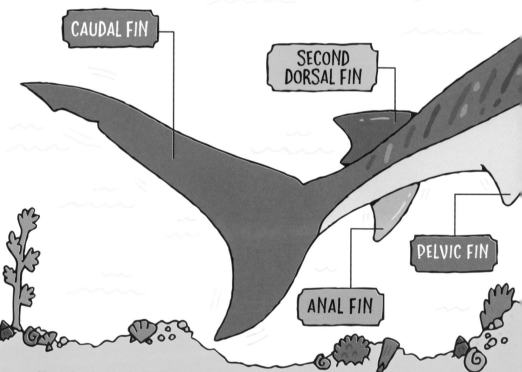

CAUDAL FIN

SECOND DORSAL FIN

PELVIC FIN

ANAL FIN

How do sharks breathe?
A shark has 5 to 7 **gills**, or slits that help it breathe, on either side of its head. Water passes through its mouth and over the gills. The shark's tiny blood vessels then pull oxygen from the water. Some sharks need to be constantly moving so water always flows through the gills. Others rely on a special part called a spiracle. The **spiracle** pumps water over the gills while a shark is lying on the seabed or buried under sand.

What does a shark use its tail for?
The tail, or **caudal fin**, works as a propeller. It pushes back and forth to speed the shark through the water. Fast sharks have firm crescent-shaped tails, and slower swimmers have longer, whip-like tails.

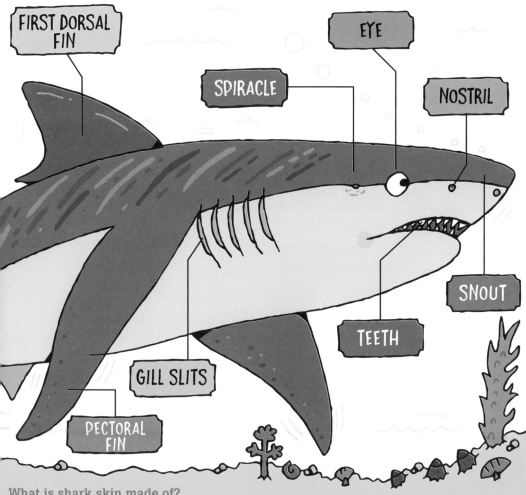

FIRST DORSAL FIN

SPIRACLE

EYE

NOSTRIL

SNOUT

TEETH

GILL SLITS

PECTORAL FIN

What is shark skin made of?
Its skin is made of tiny V-shaped plates called **denticles**. These scales reduce drag, letting a shark swim quietly and at great speed. A shark's muscles are attached to the inside of its skin, rather than its skeleton, which adds power to its movements while reinforcing its skin.

Are all sharks covered in dark gray skin?
Not at all! Many have a dark gray upper side, to blend in with water from above, and a lighter underside to merge with the brighter surface of the sea as seen from below. The strangely-named **tasselled wobbegong** has camouflaged sand-colored skin which allows it to hide on the seabed, and young **tiger sharks** have (you've guessed it) dark stripes down their backs.

FACT OR FICTION

9

How many bones does a shark's body contain?

None! Its skeleton is made of a super-tough long-lasting material called **cartilage** (it's the same stuff that shapes your ear). This makes sharks incredibly flexible, so be careful if you touch a shark's tail, as it can bend backward and bite you! Cartilage is also lightweight compared to bone, so it's no sweat for a shark to swim a long distance.

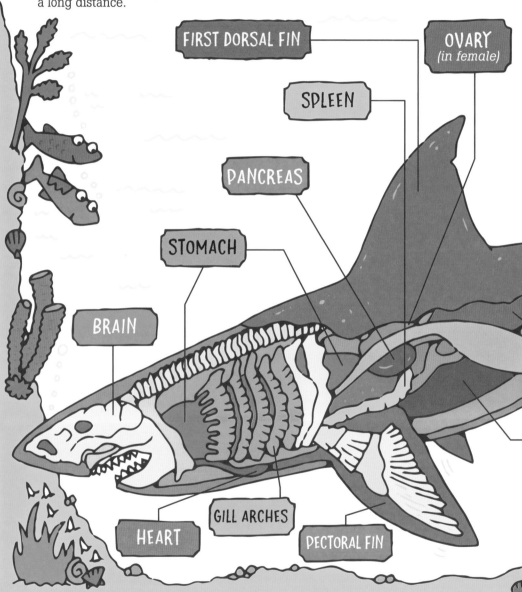

FIRST DORSAL FIN

OVARY
(in female)

SPLEEN

PANCREAS

STOMACH

BRAIN

GILL ARCHES

HEART

PECTORAL FIN

How strong are a shark's fearsome jaws?

Considering the size of their bodies, a shark's bite is actually quite weak. However, their huge jaws can be detached from their skulls, which means they can reach out and take a chunk out of their prey. Their major weaponry comes from their super-sharp teeth, with some species having more than 3,000 fangs!

FACT OR FICTION

Is a shark waterproof?

No! Water seeps in through its mouth and skin, so its kidneys spring into action to get rid of unwanted water.

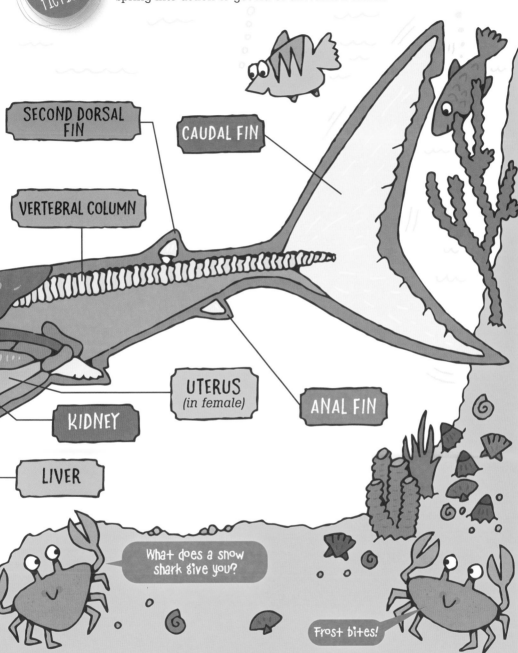

SECOND DORSAL FIN

CAUDAL FIN

VERTEBRAL COLUMN

UTERUS
(in female)

ANAL FIN

KIDNEY

LIVER

What does a snow shark give you?

Frost bites!

How do sharks stay afloat?

Most sharks need to be continually moving to stay afloat and avoid sinking to the ocean floor. However, their huge, oily **livers** keep them afloat.

BABY TALK!

It's time to take a look at the beginning of a baby shark's life. Let's see how these youngsters make a splash as they enter the ocean!

Cats have kittens, and cows have calves. What are baby sharks called? They're called **pups**!

How does a female shark become pregnant?
Once a year, male and female sharks will meet to mate. Their courtship can seem violent at times, with the male twisting around the female, while biting her fin and back. Once the male fertilizes the female's egg, "Dad" is never to be seen again.

How are baby sharks made?

There are three main ways a female shark gives birth:

1. Oviparity *(OH-vee-PAIR-ih-tee)* (egg laying)

The female produces eggs wrapped in a tough, leathery egg case, which contains all the nutrients the developing pups need. Sometimes called **mermaid's purses**, shark egg cases are made from a material called **keratin**, which is also found in your hair and fingernails. The female shark takes time to make sure her eggs are fixed in a safe place. Safety-conscious **horn sharks** wedge their screw-shaped eggs in crevices and under rocks.

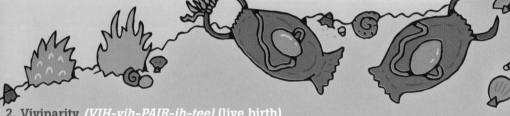

2. Viviparity *(VIH-vih-PAIR-ih-tee)* (live birth)

In this method, the pup develops inside the female shark. It gets all the oxygen and nutrients it needs through a cord that connects it to the mother shark.

3. Ovoviviparity *(OH-voh-VYE-vih-PAIR-ih-tee)* (a mix of live birth and egg laying)

Here, the female carries the eggs inside her body as an extra safety precaution against predators. The pup hatches inside its mother, who then gives birth. Some horrid **sand tiger shark** pups eat their un-hatched brothers and sisters while inside their moms.

How long does it take before a pup is ready to be born?
It depends on the species. The average pregnancy for a **great white shark** is around 12 months, while the **frilled shark** gives birth after a long 3.5 years.

How many baby sharks does one litter contain?
The number of pups varies hugely, from one or two pups
(sand tiger sharks) to around 300 at once (whale sharks).

What size are shark pups when they are born?
Let's look at the great white shark. At birth, these pups measure around 5 feet (1.5 m) in length and weigh about 50 to 60 lbs (22.7 to 27.2 kg). That's ten times heavier than an average human baby. It takes 10 to 18 years for the pup to fully mature, and they live for around 70 years.

Are all shark pups this big?
Nope! The female dwarf lantern shark gives birth to pups measuring around 2.3 in (6 cm) long. That's shorter than a crayon!

How do young shark pups survive?
Once born, they're on their own. They hunt smaller, slower prey such as little fish and squid until they grow big enough to take on larger prey. They have a cartilage tongue, or **basihyal** (BASE-ih-HIGH-yuhl), which they use to sample prey and check if it's good enough to eat.

SHARK SENSES AND SIGNALS

How do sharks get along? Do they happily hang out beneath the waves or find a solitary spot on the seabed?

There's a swarm of bees and a gaggle of geese. What is a group of sharks called? It's a **school** of sharks!

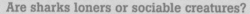

Are sharks loners or sociable creatures? A bit of both! Some sharks only work together when hunting for food or searching for a mate, and others live peacefully together in groups.

SHARK BEHAVIOR GUIDE

How do sharks communicate with each other?

Well, they can't chat to each other, but they can use body language to sort out scraps or decide who's first in the feeding line.
Take a look!

1 Why do sharks size each other up?

The biggest sharks are in charge, with the smaller ones acting as their minions.

2 Take a look at the splashing sharks. What does that mean?

Some sharks slap their tails when feeding together, perhaps to scare fellow diners away.

3 Why do sharks perform a "swim-by"?

Sharks check each other out with a slow swim-by, to see if they've met each other before or to compare sizes and establish dominance.

4 Why do sharks circle each other?

Occasionally, sharks circle each other to identify one another and establish their ranks.

5 What should I do if a shark hunches its back?

Keep clear! A shark with a raised head, hunched back, and downward pointing fins usually means "if you come any closer I'm gonna bite!"

Apart from body language, how does a shark get important information?
Like humans, sharks have the five senses of smell, hearing, touch, taste, and sight.
However, they also have an amazing extra super–sense!

Cool! Can they predict the future?
Erm…no, that's not it! It's called **electroreception**. This is an ability to detect
electricity using special cells called **ampullae** *(AM–pyoo–lay)*, which are
found under a shark's snout.

SMELL

Sharks have a fantastic sense of smell and could sniff
out one drop of blood in a small swimming pool.

SIGHT

With its eyes on different sides of its head, a shark has an almost
360–degree field of vision. Like a cat, the shark is able to see
in low light due to a mirror–like structure in the
back of its eye called the **tapetum lucidum**.

TASTE

Taste buds line a shark's mouth and throat to help it
decide whether the catch of the day is OK to swallow.

LATERAL LINE

Tiny organs detect movements and pressure changes in the water like a sense of touch. This helps sharks catch moving prey.

HEARING

Sharks have internal ears, with two tiny holes on either side of their heads. Sound travels farther and faster underwater, so sharks can detect their prey from more than 800 ft (243 m) away.

Why do sharks swim in salt water?

Because pepper water makes them sneeze!

How do sharks use electroreception?
All living animals produce a small electrical current when they move. So even when sharks are swimming in murky water or in the dark depths, they will still be able to find and catch their suppers!

Does electroreception have any other benefits?
Yep! It's a shark's GPS! They can track the earth's electromagnetic field with their built-in compass when hunting or migrating through the huge oceans.

IT'S CRUNCH TIME!

It's supper-time for sea creatures! Let's see what's on the marine menu down at the Shark Café.

What does a shark love to eat?
That all depends on the size of the shark and the shape of its teeth. Let's have a look at some examples:

Name? Great White Shark

How big is it? 15–16 ft (4.5–4.8 m) for females; 11–13 ft (3.3–3.9 m) for males

What teeth does it have? Jagged, pointed teeth

What's its favorite food? It snacks on sea lions!

Name? Shortfin Mako Shark

How big is it? 13 ft (4 m)

What teeth does it have? Backward-pointing needle-like teeth

What's its favorite food? Fast-swimming fish like tuna and billfish. It often bites their tails off first, so they can't swim away!

Name? Port Jackson Shark

How big is it? Up to 5 ft (1.5 m)

What teeth does it have? Sharp front teeth to grab its prey, then round flat teeth at the back to grind up food

What's its favorite food? It crunches down on sea urchin and crab.

Name? Basking Shark

How big is it? On average, around 22–29 ft (6.7–8.8 m)

What teeth does it have? Small teeth, as they don't chew their food. They use their long gill slits to filter their food from seawater.

What's its favorite food? They devour zooplankton, and are called filter feeders.

What are zooplankton?
They are a jumble of tiny organisms drifting in oceans
and seas, and can include krill (tiny, shrimp-like creatures), baby crabs, jellyfish, fish eggs, and tiny fish. A whale shark can digest 46 lbs (21 kg) of zooplankton every day. That's equal to 360 hot dogs!

Are sharks skillful hunters?

Sure! Take a look at some of these fiendish techniques!

Do they work as a team?
Some sharks use teamwork to swarm, confuse, and capture huge shoals of fish. Strength in numbers!

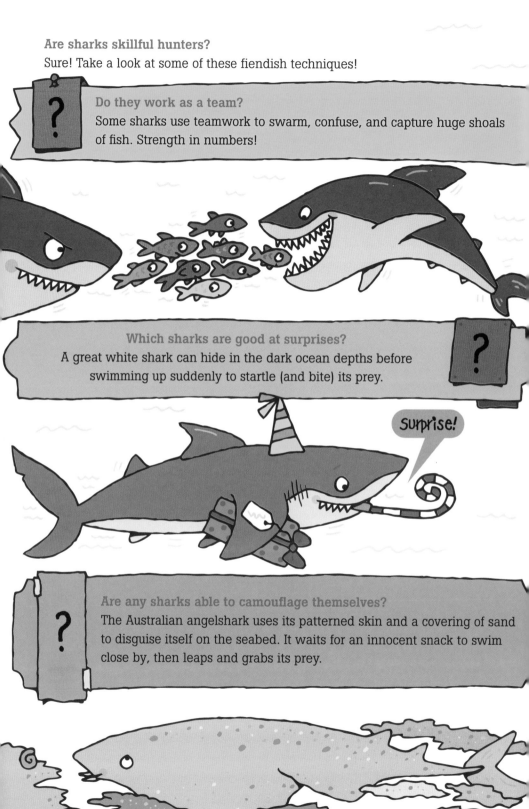

Which sharks are good at surprises?
A great white shark can hide in the dark ocean depths before swimming up suddenly to startle (and bite) its prey.

Surprise!

Are any sharks able to camouflage themselves?
The Australian angelshark uses its patterned skin and a covering of sand to disguise itself on the seabed. It waits for an innocent snack to swim close by, then leaps and grabs its prey.

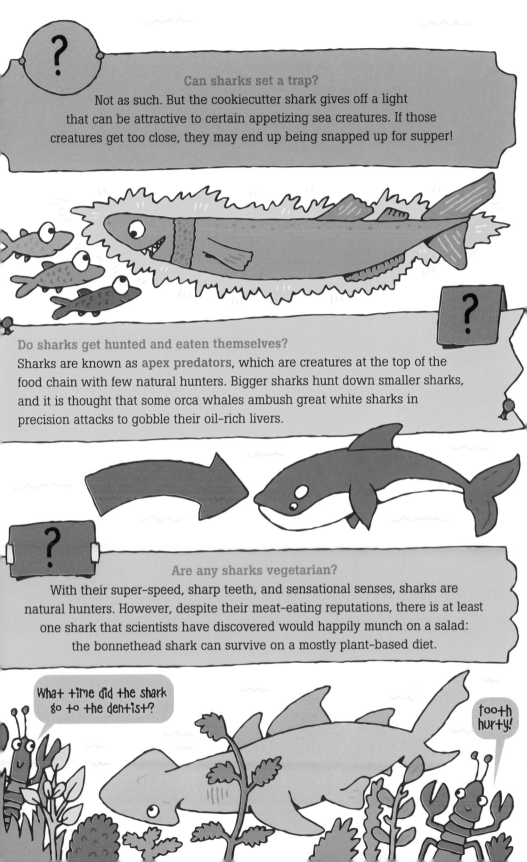

Can sharks set a trap?
Not as such. But the cookiecutter shark gives off a light
that can be attractive to certain appetizing sea creatures. If those
creatures get too close, they may end up being snapped up for supper!

Do sharks get hunted and eaten themselves?
Sharks are known as **apex predators**, which are creatures at the top of the
food chain with few natural hunters. Bigger sharks hunt down smaller sharks,
and it is thought that some orca whales ambush great white sharks in
precision attacks to gobble their oil-rich livers.

Are any sharks vegetarian?
With their super-speed, sharp teeth, and sensational senses, sharks are
natural hunters. However, despite their meat-eating reputations, there is at least
one shark that scientists have discovered would happily munch on a salad:
the bonnethead shark can survive on a mostly plant-based diet.

What time did the shark
go to the dentist?

tooth
hurty!

SHARK ATTACK!

Let's sort out the facts from the fiction. Is it safe to surf the waves and splash along the seashore?

What are my chances of getting snapped at by a shark?

Unprovoked shark attacks are very rare. Around 50 to 80 incidents happen worldwide each year, giving you a 1 in 11.5 million chance of an unpleasant shark encounter.

Cool! So, sharks don't really enjoy sniffing out humans to snack on?

Far from it. Only 30 species of shark have ever attacked a human. Even then, a shark may have been attracted by splashing feet or light catching a piece of jewelry and confused the human with a natural food source. The United States averages just 40 shark attacks each year, with one fatality every two years.

Are shark attacks more common at any particular time?

Sharks feed at dawn and dusk, so it's best to avoid swimming at these times. In Florida, where most U.S. attacks occur, September is the most dangerous month.

Are there any famous shark survival stories?

One of the first recorded shark attacks took place in Havana Bay, Cuba, in 1749. Fourteen-year-old English cabin boy Brook Watson went for a swim in the harbor and was attacked twice by a shark, who bit off his right foot at the ankle. He survived, but he lost his leg as a result. Watson went on to become a prominent politician!

WANTED

I SURVIVED!

TOP TIPS!

What should I do to avoid a face-to-face meeting with a surly shark?

1 **Stay in a group.** Sharks are more likely to attack if you're on your own.

2 **Don't swim too far away from the shore.** This makes you vulnerable and puts you far away from help.

3 **Avoid the water at night, dawn, or dusk.**

4 **If you're bleeding from a cut, don't get in the water.** A shark may sniff you out.

5 **Remove shiny jewelry.** The sparkly light may attract a shark.

What do you call the mushy stuff between a shark's teeth?

Slow swimmers!

6 Don't splash too much, or allow a pet to jump around you. These sudden movements may get a shark's attention.

7 Avoid wearing a brightly colored swimsuit, and watch out if your tan isn't even. Sharks can spot contrasting colors!

8 Don't swim with a lot of fish or in areas where people are fishing. Schools and bait attract sharks!

9 Don't enter the water if you know that sharks are present. If you spot a shark, keep your eyes on the creature and calmly exit the water without making any sudden movements.

In the unlikely event of an attack, how should I behave?
Take action! Hit the shark as hard as you can on the nose. This might give you some time to get out of the water.

WHERE IN THE WORLD?

Sharks live almost anywhere underwater. Let's take a tour of the places a shark calls home.

Which of the oceans do sharks live in?
All five! Sharks can be found in the Atlantic, Pacific, Indian, Arctic, and Southern Oceans.

Can sharks survive only in saltwater?
Not true! Some species can be found in freshwater lakes and rivers. The **bull shark**, for instance, swims huge distances up the Amazon River.

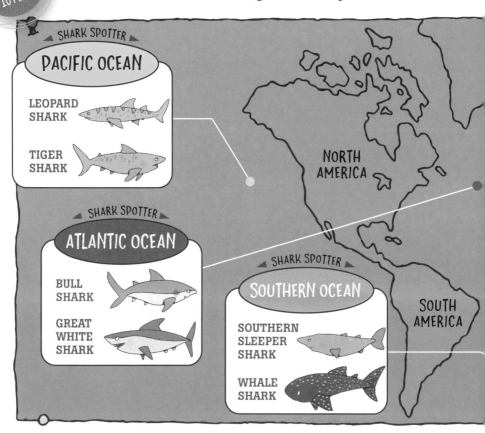

Which sharks live in shallow water?
Nurse sharks survive in warm, coastal waters, where they hunt their prey in the sandy seabed.

Are sharks found in coral reefs?
Sure! Some call the reef home and others just pop by to hunt for food. The **whitetip reef shark** dozes all day, then hunts in packs at night. They target fish that are hiding in the reef's cracks and crevices.

How do sharks survive in the open ocean?

In the open ocean meals can be scarce, so sharks need their super senses to locate their prey. The **oceanic whitetip shark** feeds on bony fish, stingrays, sea turtles, seabirds, and dead whales. It can even detect the sound of fishing boat engines and can steal fish straight off their lines!

Which sharks live on the sea floor?

Do you remember the camouflaged **angelshark**? With their skin mimicking the color and pattern of the sand, these sharks are hard to spot. They're not alone, either! **Wobbegongs** nestle on the sea floor to wait for prey, just like angelsharks, and **zebra sharks** and **sawsharks** can also be found if you look hard enough.

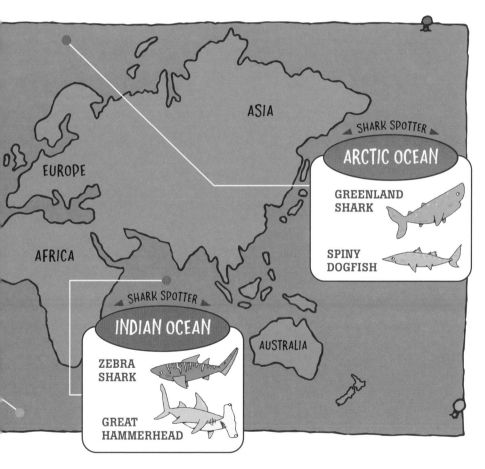

ASIA

EUROPE

AFRICA

◄ SHARK SPOTTER ►
ARCTIC OCEAN

GREENLAND SHARK

SPINY DOGFISH

◄ SHARK SPOTTER ►
INDIAN OCEAN

AUSTRALIA

ZEBRA SHARK

GREAT HAMMERHEAD

What characteristics have deep sea sharks developed?

In the dark cold depths of the deep sea, some sharks glow, and others have developed huge eyes that detect tiny glimmers of light. The recently discovered **ninja lanternshark** is a mere 20 inches (51 cm) long, but boasts pale green glowing organs that both attract and confuse its prey.

Do sharks stay in the same place they were born?
Many sharks do. However, some larger sharks swim huge distances
on epic journeys called **migrations**.

Why do sharks migrate?
Some sharks want to stay in warmer water, so they move
with the seasons. Other sharks travel to find a mate, or make incredible
journeys to sniff out the top feeding spots.

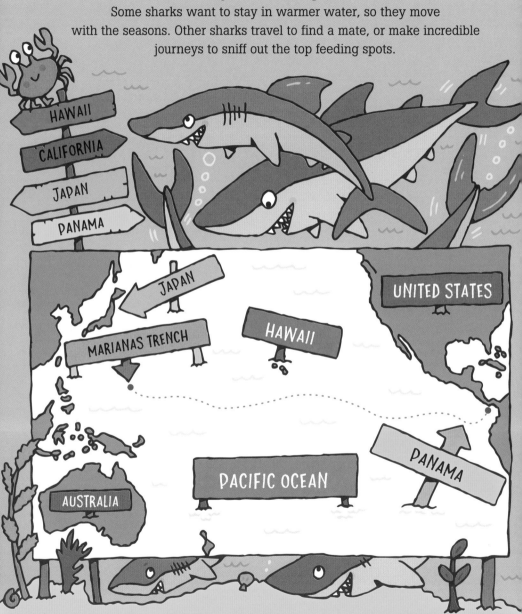

How far do some sharks travel?
A record-breaking whale shark took nearly two-and-a-half years to swim over
12,000 miles (20,000 km) from Panama to the Marianas Trench. Female whale
sharks are steady swimmers, and can cover around 42 miles (67 km) each day.

Do we know why sharks go where they go?

Some shark behavior is puzzling. Each winter, a mass of great white sharks leave California and travel the 2,490 miles (4,000 km) to Hawaii, then make the return journey in late spring. In between, they head to a massive area nicknamed **The White Shark Café**. Here, the male sharks make hundreds of dives a day to depths of over 1,000 feet. Scientists are working to discover the reason for these dives. Could they be diving for a specific fish or to impress a potential mate?

How do migrating sharks know where to go?

It's thought that most sharks use their acute sense of smell, travel by a navigation system using their electroreception, or make a mental map of the ocean floor.

UNDERWATER IDENTITY PARADE!

If you think you know what a shark looks like, you may be surprised! Not all sharks appear the same, so let's get the lowdown on the different categories.

What do bramble sharks have in common with prickly sharks?
Both types of sharks are the only two species left in the **Echinorhinidae** *(EH-kee-noh-RHY-nih-day)* family. They're slow-swimming, deep-dwelling, well-armored sharks that get their names from the thorn-like **denticles** covering their thin skin.

1 ECHINORHINIDAE SHARKS

Rough skin covered in sharp, pointy denticles

EXHIBIT

Bramble Shark

What's so amazing about the cow shark and frilled shark gangs?
These groups are filled with the oldest and most primitive sharks. They inhabit the cold deep ocean, but sometimes venture into cool coastal seas. In fact, the **broadnose sevengill shark** can survive in as little as 4 ft (1 m) of water!

COW AND FRILLED SHARKS 2

Look! Seven gills!

EXHIBIT

Broadnose Sevengill Shark

Do bullhead sharks live up to their name?

Pretty much! They feature big heads with large snouts and a crest above their eyes. Some species even charge along the seabed using their pectoral and pelvic fins.

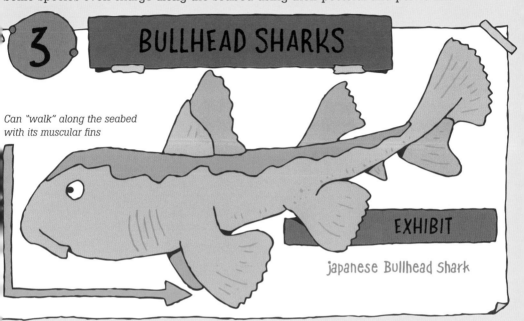

3

BULLHEAD SHARKS

Can "walk" along the seabed with its muscular fins

EXHIBIT

japanese Bullhead Shark

How did carpet sharks get their name?

Most species in this group feature a colorful patterned skin and fringed edges. Many live on the ocean floor, just like a carpet on the seabed. The shy **necklace carpet shark** only comes out at night and has a dark collar with dense, white spots, hence its name!

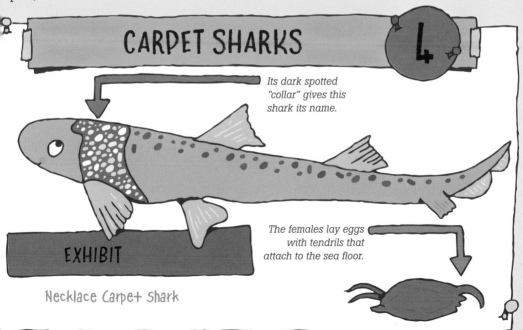

CARPET SHARKS

4

Its dark spotted "collar" gives this shark its name.

The females lay eggs with tendrils that attach to the sea floor.

EXHIBIT

Necklace Carpet Shark

Do mackerel sharks have anything to do with mackerel, the fish?
Yes! They got their name from the fact that many species eat schools of smaller fish, like mackerel. The **pelagic thresher shark** uses its whip-like tail to stun small fish before gobbling them whole.

5 MACKEREL SHARKS

Knock-out tail

EXHIBIT

Pelagic thresher Shark

Why is a dogfish shark called a dogfish?
Dogfish sharks, which include the **spiny dogfish** (one of the most common sharks in the world), are called that because they hunt in packs, just like dogs!

What sorts of sharks are in the dogfish tribe?
There are 130 different kinds of dogfish swimming in the Earth's oceans.

DOGFISH SHARKS

Each dorsal fin features a sharp, poisonous spike.

EXHIBIT

Spiny Dogfish

6

Which is the largest shark group?
Almost half of all shark species belong to the **ground shark** gang. That covers over 227 species, including the gigantic **bull sharks**, the slender **catshark**, and the unique-looking **hammerhead**.

7 GROUND SHARKS

Its head is actually called a cephalofoil

EXHIBIT

Frilled Hammerhead Shark

How can angelsharks remain perfectly still on the seabed?

Many sharks need to swim constantly to breathe. However, the **angelshark**, the only shark in its own group, has muscles that pump water over its gills and through the spiracles (holes) in its head. This allows it to laze on the seabed or hide for hours, then ambush its prey.

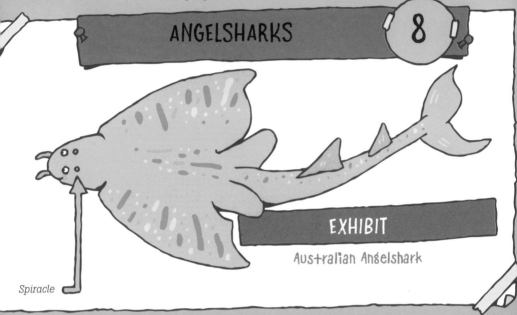

ANGELSHARKS

8

EXHIBIT

Australian Angelshark

Spiracle

What's the last group of sharks called?

Here come the **sawsharks**! These strange-looking creatures are easily recognizable with their lengthy saw-like snouts, which have sharp teeth poking out from either side. They slash this "saw" from side to side, hacking into their intended prey. Sounds gruesome!

9

SAWSHARK SHARKS

EXHIBIT

Longnose Sawshark

It uses its teeth to stir up sand, then attack its prey.

OCEAN-FLOOR FREAK SHOW!

The deep ocean is home to some weird and wonderful specimens. Let's take a long dive and spot some strange-looking sharks!

What is this sinister-looking shark?

It's the **goblin shark**. That long, pointy snout is packed with sense organs, which comes in handy when searching for its supper in deep dark water. Its jaw can extend out as far as the tip of its nose, which helps the shark snap at squid, crab, and crayfish.

Who is the shark with the gigantic jaw?

Introducing the **megamouth shark**! This specimen measures an average 16 ft (5 m) long, with a mouth that's around 4 ft (1.3 m) across. That's as wide as 3 bowling pins end to end! It is thought that their lips can glow to attract plankton.

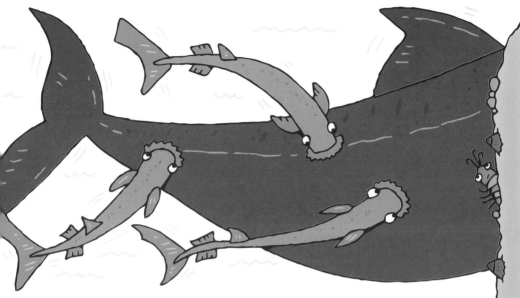

How did the cookiecutter shark get its name?
The **cookiecutter shark** attaches itself to much larger prey with its strong suction lips, then spins its body, using its teeth to cut out a cookie-shaped plug of flesh. Dinner is served!

What is this odd exhibit? It looks almost prehistoric!
It's a **frilled shark**. Known as a "living fossil," it's thought to have been around for at least 80 million years! Scientists believe this creature has remained mostly unchanged since the Cretaceous Period, when dinosaurs still roamed the planet. With its 300 razor-sharp teeth, I wouldn't hang around to ask it too many questions about the dinosaurs!

Here comes the dwarf lantern shark! What is its claim to fame?
It's the world's smallest shark. This tiny specimen is smaller than
a human hand but still manages to pack in oversized eyes
and plenty of glow-in-the-dark organs!

What's a shark's favorite TV show?

LANTERN SHARK REUNION

Whale of Fortune!

Is the dwarf lantern shark related to the ninja lantern shark?
Yes! The family also includes the **velvet belly shark**,
and they all have one thing in common: they glow!

What's the most mysterious shark?

It's not every day that you dive down nearly 6,500 ft (2,000 m),
so it's rare to bump into some of these sharks. Little is known about the
spookily-named ghost catshark or demon catshark, apart from the
odd specimen caught accidentally by deep-sea fishing.

What's with the nose on this guy?

That's the bluntnose sixgill shark, or cow shark for short! This shark can grow
to an average length of 16 ft (4.8 m) long, and feeds on dolphinfish, flounder,
rays, and even other sharks. It can be found at depths reaching
8,000 ft (2,500 m). Its broad, rounded nose (and six gills,
for that matter) are its signature features!

SALTWATER SUPERSTARS!

Time to hand out some sea life awards. Let's take a look at the sharks that rule the waves!

Who wins the fastest shark award?

The gold medal goes to the **shortfin mako shark**, which reaches speeds of over 43 miles per hour (69 kph). It still has a way to go to beat the fastest sea animal (the sensational sailfish, which swims over 10 miles per hour/40 kph faster).

Which shark lives the longest?

The old-timers' award is handed to the **Greenland shark**. This senior specimen can live as long as 400 years, with an average lifespan of 272 years. That's a lot of birthdays! These sharks take their time to mature, and grow at an extremely slow half an inch (1 cm) per year!

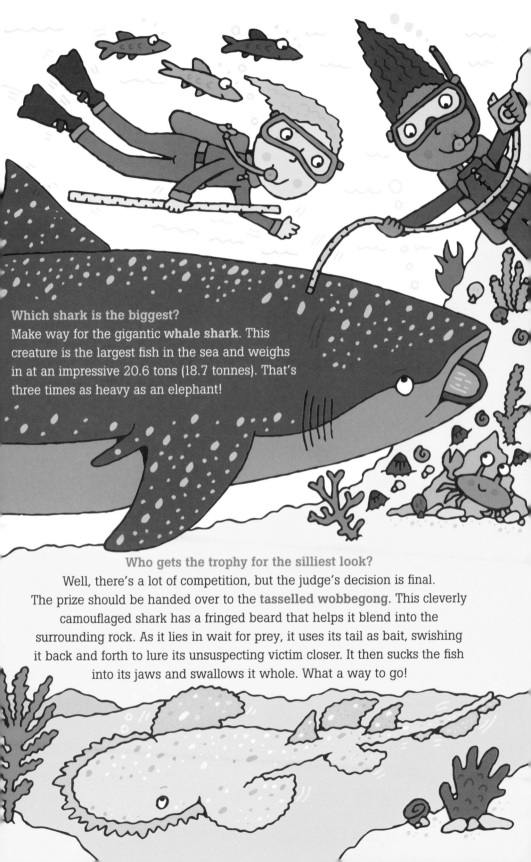

Which shark is the biggest?
Make way for the gigantic **whale shark**. This creature is the largest fish in the sea and weighs in at an impressive 20.6 tons (18.7 tonnes). That's three times as heavy as an elephant!

Who gets the trophy for the silliest look?
Well, there's a lot of competition, but the judge's decision is final. The prize should be handed over to the **tasselled wobbegong**. This cleverly camouflaged shark has a fringed beard that helps it blend into the surrounding rock. As it lies in wait for prey, it uses its tail as bait, swishing it back and forth to lure its unsuspecting victim closer. It then sucks the fish into its jaws and swallows it whole. What a way to go!

Which shark has the strongest bite?

The **great white shark**! Its powerful jaws exert an incredible force of 2 tons (1.8 tonnes), which is roughly 20 times stronger than what a human's bite can do.

GREAT WHITE SHARK

Who gets the hazardous honor for the sharpest teeth?

It's a tie! To figure this out, scientists have made power saws fitted with shark teeth to test their cutting capability. The **tiger** and **silky sharks** owned the sharpest gnashers, but the **bluenose sixgill's** teeth lasted the longest. We'll try and fit all three on the winner's podium!

SILKY SHARK

TIGER SHARK

BLUENOSE SIXGILL

NO BITING!

Which shark gets the gold for the largest fin?
The **common thresher shark** has a tail fin that's almost half the length of its whole body! This helps it hunt by giving it a handy whip for knocking out its prey!

WATCH OUT!

COMMON THRESHER SHARK

Which shark is the cleverest?
That's not easy to answer, as they haven't all taken the same test! The brains of **scalloped hammerhead sharks** are unusually large for a shark their size, which might explain both their sharpened senses and how well they get along in a group. However, the **great white shark** also has highly developed senses, *and* is clever enough to outfox its prey of brainy seals and dolphins.

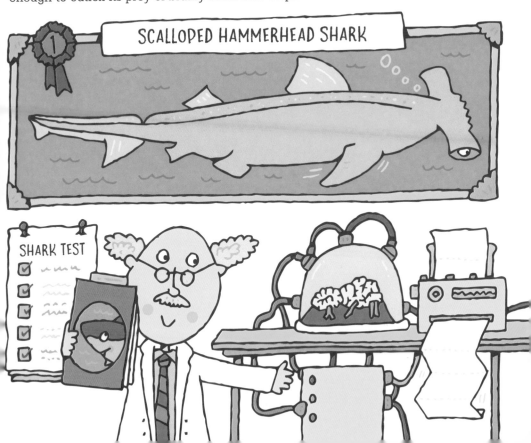

SCALLOPED HAMMERHEAD SHARK

SHARK TEST

FANG-TASTIC SHARK FACTS!

Time to get myth-busting! Let's jump in and get the inside scoop on these magnificent creatures.

Do sharks sleep?

Sort of! Sharks don't sleep as we know it. Instead, they enter restful periods, or periods where they're only *partly* awake. This allows sharks to keep moving, even when their brains are at rest!

How can you tell how old a shark is?

In some shark species, you can count "growth layers" in their spines—sort of like counting rings on a tree trunk! Another way is to take a look at how old the shark's eye lens is, because it was formed before the animal was born.

Do sharks make sounds?

Sharks are known as silent hunters because they don't possess body parts that can make sounds, such as vocal cords, so they're unable to make noises like other animals. The closest thing to a noise that sharks make is the barking a **draughts-board shark** makes when it surfaces, but this is from air being released from their bodies (in self-defense) when pulled out of the water.

Do great white sharks need to eat every day?

Not at all! They store energy in their livers! This allows them to make migrations across thousands of miles of open ocean without stopping.

Can sharks swim backward?

No! Unlike other fish, sharks' pectoral fins cannot bend upward, so they have to keep moving forward. Never try and pull a shark backward either. Water can get into their gills and make them drown!

What do you get when you cross a great white shark with a trumpet fish?

Can sharks live out of water?

Let's look at the epaulette shark. Not only can this one-of-a-kind creature use its fins to crawl over rock pools, but it can also survive for short periods out of the sea. It can go without oxygen for at least three hours. This lets the adaptable shark hunt in exposed reefs!

Dunno...but I don't want to play it!

Is some shark meat poisonous?

Yes! Most shark meat contains high levels of mercury, a metal that, when eaten, can mess with your nervous system—even kill you.

Are sharks related to stingrays?

Yes—they share many similarities. Both have skeletons made of cartilage, and unlike other fish, they have no swim bladders. Both species have teeth in rows and five to seven pairs of gills. Rays, unlike sharks, move their pectoral fins to swim.

SAVE OUR SHARKS!

It may be a top predator, but the shark is under serious threat. Let's get up to speed on the threats to these spectacular creatures.

What is the biggest danger facing sharks?

Humans. It is thought that 100 million sharks are killed every single year. Sharks are overfished to supply the huge demand for their fins, which are used in expensive delicacies throughout Asia, or they're accidentally caught in fishing gear meant for other species. Sharks are also losing important nursery and feeding grounds as humans cut down mangroves and destroy coral reefs.

Why is this allowed to happen?

There is very little management or control. There are laws to protect sharks and ban the sale of their fins, but these aren't widespread enough. Often, nothing stops people from illegally fishing for sharks, and some fishing techniques meant for other fish, such as trawling or longlines, scoop sharks up too.

Which species are under threat?

Sharks are slow-growing and slow to reproduce, so they're incredibly vulnerable. The **scalloped hammerhead shark** has declined by 99 percent in some parts of the ocean over the last 30 years. Stocks of the **silky shark** have halved since the 1970s, and even the great white shark is now vulnerable to extinction.

Is there anything we can do to improve this dire situation?

We can boycott shark meat as well as any products that may contain shark oil or cartilage, and we can be more careful and eat only seafood fished or farmed using eco-responsible methods. Also, we can look after the ocean by recycling and reducing our use of plastics. The more we educate ourselves and others about these magnificent creatures, the more we can help save them.

CHECK OUT ALL OF THE FANTASTIC FACTS IN THIS SENSATIONAL SERIES!

100 Questions about Bugs

100 Questions about Colonial America

100 Questions about Dinosaurs

100 Questions about the Human Body

100 Questions about Oceans

100 Questions about Outer Space

100 Questions about Pirates

100 Questions about Sharks